Help Me Understand...

A guide to help children understand hospitals, death, and organ, cornea & tissue donation

Written by: Michelle Post, MA, LMFT, CTBS
Illustrations by: Karin Stothart, MFA, CTBS

Help me understand. A workbook for grieving children and those who love them.
Written by Michelle A. Post, MA, LMFT, CTBS. Illustrations by Karin Stothart, MFA, CTBS

Copyright 2022, Michelle A. Post, MA, LMFT
Published and distributed by Post International Services, Inc.
www.PostInternationalinc.com, michelle@postinternationalinc.com, (213) 373-5037

ISBN: 978-1-7331086-2-1

Dedications

To all the families who I've been with during the most difficult times of their lives, giving news that no child should have to hear, "Someone close to you has died": Thank you for inspiring me with your resiliency.

To my colleagues through NACG, AOPO, AATB, and ADEC, especially my mentors, J. William Worden, Ph.D. and William "Bill" Hoy, D. Min.: Thank you for your wisdom and guidance.

To my own late father, Rev. Howard E. Post, for your inspiration: I am who I am because of your triumphs and in spite of your struggles, and I miss you. And to my surviving family -- my mother, Carolyn, brother, Nathan, and sister-in-law, Lynda: In the face of your own grief, losses, and changes, you showed honesty, integrity, sadness, anger, happiness, relief, shock, faith, and courage. Thank you for modeling such tenacity and grace, and thank you for your love.

And to Brian Wannberg, RN, transplant coordinator, lung-transplant biotech genius, my chef, confidant, and love of my life: Thank you for the times you helped me in and out of hospitals to provide compassionate care for the families of organ, eye, and tissue donors. I especially appreciate your support through the harrowing trials of my father's death and the bumps and bruises of my own grief journey. I'll never forget that you remembered the TSA screwdriver confiscation. I love you.

Note to parents, guardians, and caregivers:

If you have found this book, your desire to support and protect your child is admirable. Chances are you have never needed support like this before and didn't know how to handle this situation. Thank you for reaching out for help. The research of J. William Worden, Ph.D and my actual experience with death notification and grief support for children and teens since 2003 has shown me that what will help children in the long run is to:

1. Tell children the truth about what has happened. Meaning, say that someone has died (i.e., their body stopped working, thinking, feeling, etc.), use the real medical terms (i.e., cancer, heart disease, depression/suicide, head trauma, etc.), and avoid using common phrases (i.e., "lost", "loss", "sick", "went to sleep" or explanations that involve God, heaven, or angels). Otherwise, this can confuse children and create other problems.

2. Support all of the child's feelings of anger, sadness, relief, playful/happiness, and worry (because these are normal reactions). Avoid telling them to "be strong", which they interpret as "don't feel". Share your feelings with them because you are their biggest role model of how to grieve in a healthy way. Also, after someone dies, children are often afraid something will happen to their caregivers and that no one will take care of them. Reassure them who will take care of them if anything happens to you, and remind them of all the things you do to take care of yourself (seatbelt, healthy eating, doctor visits, etc.).

3. Let them know it's not their fault and remind them of this from time to time.

4. Once you have prepared them for what they will see, hear, touch, smell, and experience, give them a choice to be included in the hospital visits, viewing the body, funeral/memorial planning and attendance, and cemetery visits. Bring another adult for each young child. Assign that adult to care for the child during the events and to be truthful and supportive at each event. Pack an activity bag for each child. Make sure all people involved know that the child's desire to write, draw, or play during these events are normal and not disrespectful of the deceased or the grieving family. Children who are included do better in the long run than those who are not included.

5. Check in with the child, debrief after each experience, and make a plan to check in once a week for 2 years.

6. Consider finding a grief support group for them 3-12 months after the death. For referrals to programs in your area see www.childrengrief.org or www.adec.org.

Remember that the number one predictor of how well the child will cope is to make sure their caregivers are coping well, getting support, and are physically and emotionally healthy. If you are the child's caregiver or guardian, please remember to love and care for yourself and model this for your child.

Thank you, again, for the courage to reach out for support and information.

- Michelle

Table of Contents

Help Me Understand...
What Happened in My Family

This book is about you and your family. Share a little bit about yourself and your family.

My name is _____

And I am _____ years old. My birthdate is _____

Here is a picture of my family:

Glue or tape a picture of your family, or draw a picture of your family on this page.
Write in the name of each person around the picture.

2

Something scary, sad or difficult has happened to my family.

The event or experience happened to _____

(Name or names of people involved in the accident, event or illness)

I call this person (or these people) _____

This happened on _____ (day, month, year)

Here is what happened
(write or draw what you saw or were told happened)

Help Me Understand... 5 Senses

5 Senses

When something difficult or hard happens to people, especially kids and families, sometimes it helps to draw about all of your memories using each of your 5 senses. Your 5 senses are 1) Sight, 2) Hearing, 3) Touch, 4) Taste and 5) Smell. When the difficult thing happened to you, write or draw what you remember –

seeing

words sounds **hearing**

Today's date is _____

 touching

 tasting

 smelling

Today's date is _____

7

Help Me Understand... Hospitals

Hospitals

Hospitals are special places where doctors and nurses and caring people try to help others who are really, really hurt or sick. Sometimes it's a place to go when someone needs surgery or a check up. Sometimes it's a place people go when a baby needs to be born.

What questions do you have about hospitals? Have you ever seen a hospital in your neighborhood or seen a hospital on TV or in a movie? If so, write or draw your questions or your version of the hospital you saw here:

Today's date is _____

Ambulance

Sometime people drive there, and other times an ambulance takes someone to the hospital or emergency room. An ambulance is a special fast van with medical people on board to help.

Have you ever seen or heard an ambulance? Did someone you know go to the hospital by riding in an ambulance? What questions do you have about what happened? Write or draw about what you heard, saw, smelled, touched or tasted that day the person you know went to the hospital in an ambulance.

Today's date is _____

In the Hospital: Who Was There

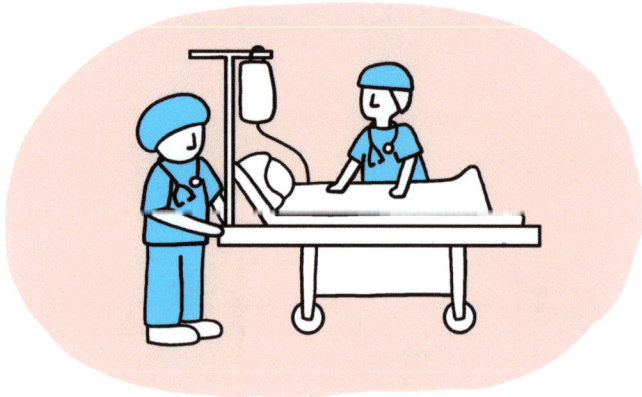

Sometimes when people go to a hospital for help or visit a person in the hospital, they see security guards, nurses, doctors, other people, and different machines that help a person's body. Write or draw your answers to these three questions:

Did you go to the hospital for help?   **YES**   **NO**
(If Yes, for what _____)

Did you go to a hospital to visit a person you know?   **YES**   **NO**
(If Yes, who _____)

What questions do you have about the hospital, who was there, what was there, or what happened there?

Today's date is _____

In the Hospital: Your 5 Senses

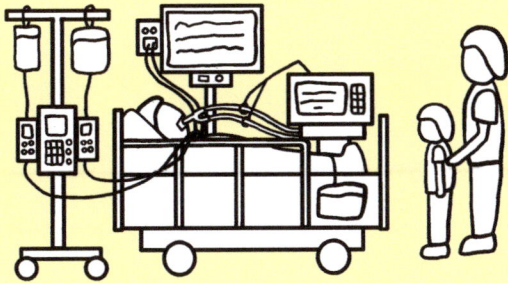

If you did go to a hospital, write or draw about what you heard, saw, smelled, touched or tasted that day when you went. If you didn't go, write or draw what you might have seen, or smelled.

Today's date is _____

Feelings

When someone you know is in the hospital, you can feel many different feelings at the same time. These can be mad, sad, happy, scared, relieved and many more. Draw a picture or write a little bit about what feelings you have:

Sad Feelings

Did you feel sad when you went to the hospital or do you remember ever feeling sad? Draw a picture or write about a time when you felt sad feelings:

Today's date is _____

Feeling Mad or Angry

Did you feel mad or angry when you went to the hospital or do you remember ever feeling mad? Draw a picture or write about a time when you felt mad feelings:

Today's date is _____

Feeling Scared or Afraid

Did you feel scared or afraid when you went to the hospital or do you ever remember ever feeling scared? Draw a picture or write about a time when you felt afraid or scared:

Feeling Happy or Relieved

Did you feel happy or relieved when you went to the hospital or do you ever remember ever feeling happy? Draw a picture or write about a time when you felt happy or relieved:

Today's date is _____

Hospital Machines

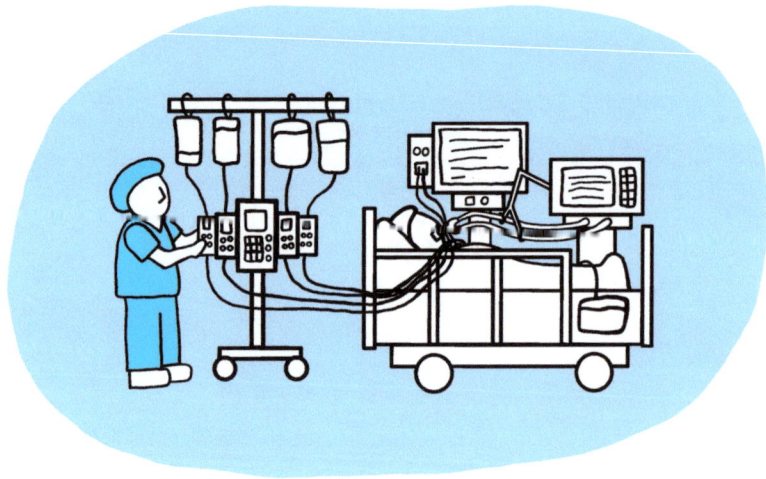

Many times people who go to the hospital for a surgery or illness come back home healthy. Sometimes so much happens at the hospital that people forget to explain to you what happened in a hospital, and what machines were needed to help someone who was in the hospital.

If you visited someone in the hospital, you may have seen different machines and heard noises like beeps, and whooshing sounds, or soft pumping sounds. The next few pages will explain many different machines that people use in the hospital to help someone's body heal.

Take a few minutes here to write or draw what machines you remember seeing or hearing, and any questions you might have about hospital machines.

Today's date is _____

Hospital Machines: Blood Pressure Monitor

When someone is hospitalized or has a really, really serious injury or illness, there is often a plastic cuff or wire attached to a fingertip that has a red light on it to check for oxygen in the blood. This is called a pulse oximeter. On babies it's sometimes attached to a foot or toe. This checks how much oxygen is in the body and is attached to another machine that sometimes beeps as it checks. This doesn't hurt the person and feels like when someone gently holds your finger.

Here is a picture of one

What questions do you have about blood pressure or blood pressure monitors?

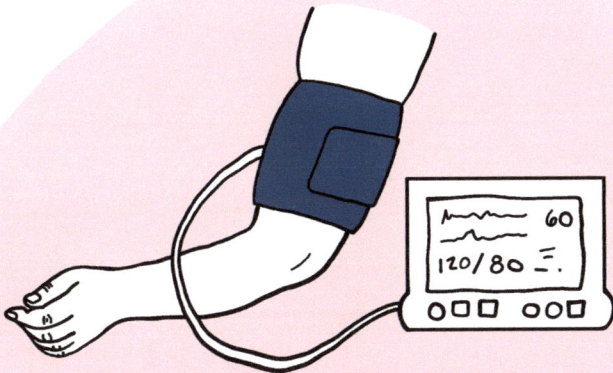

Today's date is _____

Hospital Machines: IV Drip and Monitor

When our body is healthy, it makes all the nutrients we need to keep our heart and body working. When our body needs to have surgery or when it has a serious illness or injury at the hospital, we might need special tubes call an IV drip (IV stands for intravenous = into veins). To slowly drip medicine into our body. These tubes are attached to a bag of medicine that is hung on a metal holder and attached to a machine to tell nurses when it needs adjusting.

Here is a picture

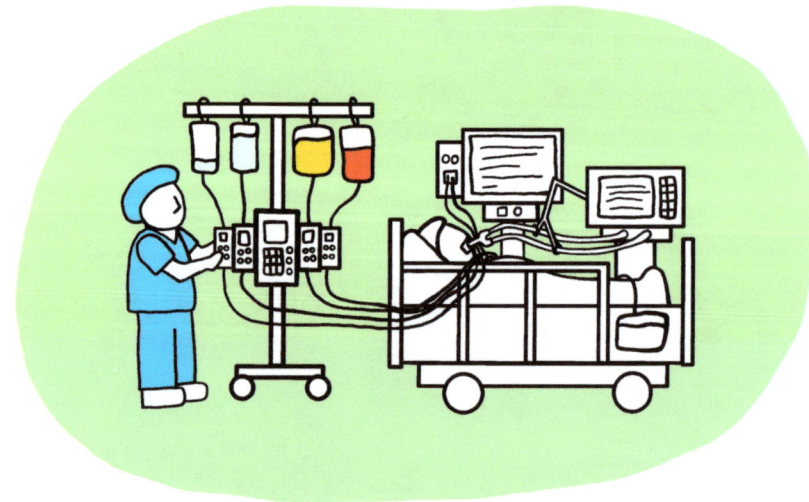

This is a close-up picture of an IV drip and monitor with many different medicines.

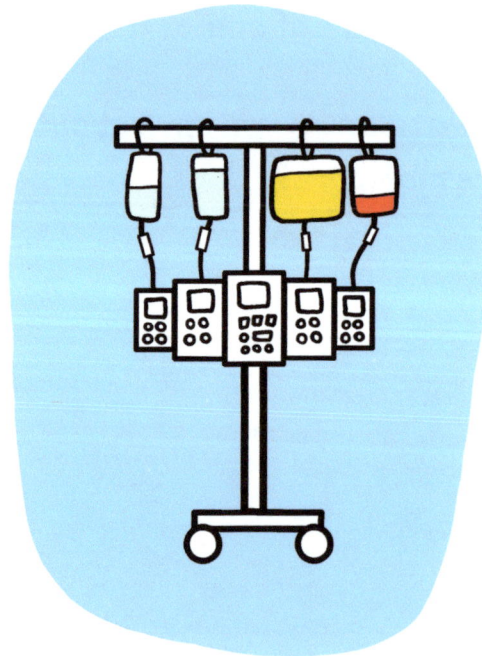

Today's date is _____

Hospital Machines: IV

Here is a close-up picture of someone's hand with an IV attached to it.

When it's put in, it stings a little like when you get a shot. But after it's in, it doesn't hurt.

What questions do you have about the IV, or medicines on the IV monitor?

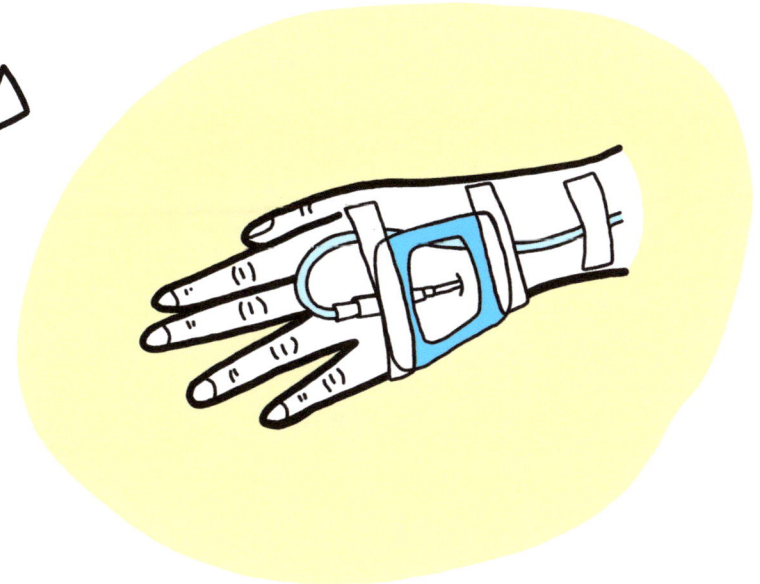

Today's date is _____

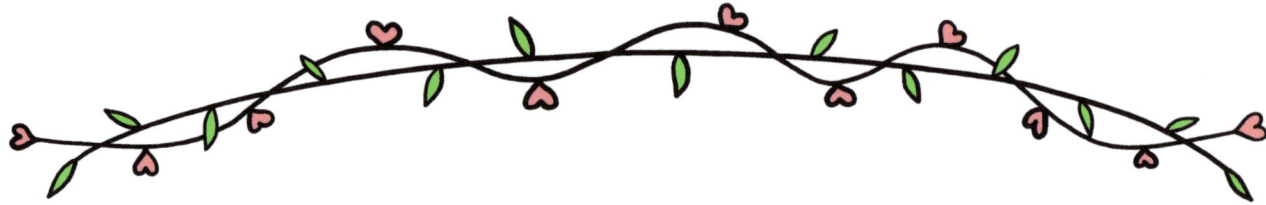

Hospital Machines: Cooling or Warming Blanket

Sometimes patients in the hospital need a machine attached to a puffy plastic blanket that cools or warms them if their body temperature changes too much. The machine again makes a sound when it's inflating the puffy blanket.

Puffy Blanket

The machine often looks like this

What questions do you have about this machine?

Today's date is _____

Hospital Machines: The Ventilator

Oxygen... the body needs oxygen to live and when our lungs are working, our lungs breathe in oxygen from the air for us.

When someone's lungs are not working well, the hospital workers help the person breathe by using a ventilator. The ventilator blows oxygen into the lungs, like when we blow air into a balloon. When someone's lungs can't breathe at all for them and they die in the hospital, their body might still be connected to the ventilator. The family can ask for the ventilator to stay on for a little while to give other people time to visit and say goodbye. But, the person's lungs and body is no longer working. Only the machines are working and blow air into the lungs like when someone blows up a balloon. The ventilator blows oxygen into the body which may keep the heart working and body warm for a few hours while people can say goodbye.

What questions do you have about oxygen, lungs, breathing or ventilators?

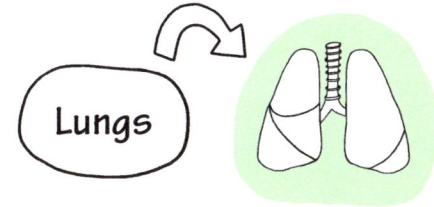

Lungs

Today's date is _____

Hospital Machines: Pulse Oximeter

When someone is hospitalized or has a really, really serious injury or illness, there is often a plastic cuff or wire attached to a fingertip that has a red light on it to check for oxygen in the blood. This is called a pulse oximeter. On babies it's sometimes attached to a foot or toe. This checks how much oxygen is in the body and is attached to another machine that sometimes beeps as it checks. This doesn't hurt the person and feels like when someone gently holds your finger.

Here is a picture of a pulse oximeter ⇨

What questions do you have about pulse oximeters?

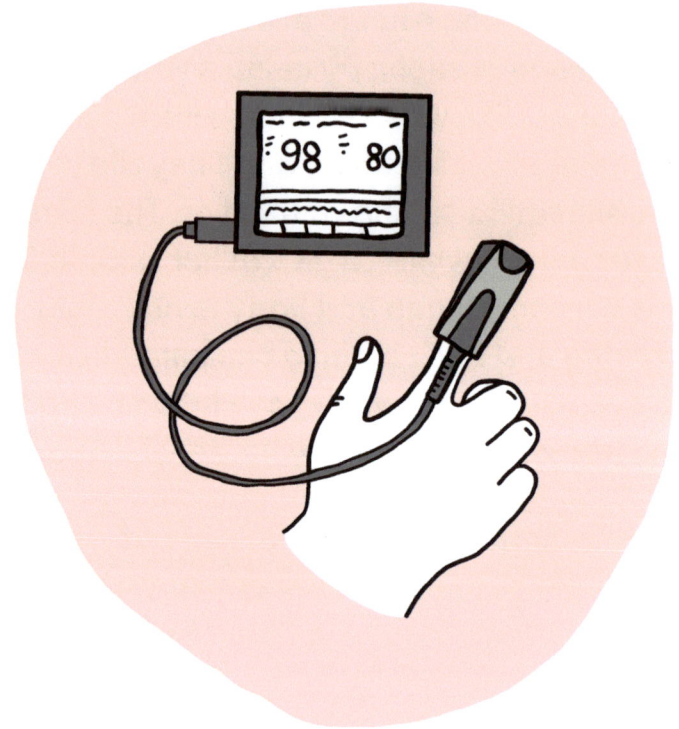

Today's date is _____

Feelings Check

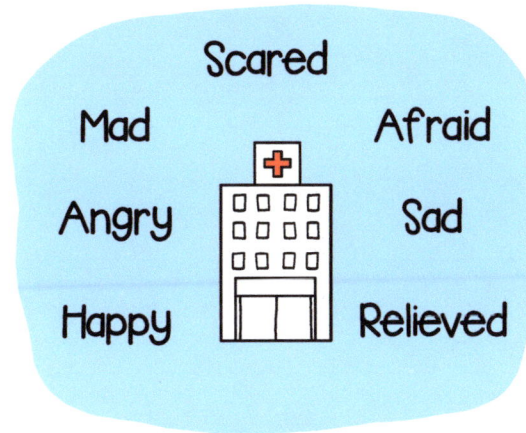

Scared

Mad   Afraid

Angry   Sad

Happy   Relieved

Just like things change in the weather as summer, fall, winter and spring seasons pass, feelings change over time and much faster than the weather or the seasons. Now that you have had some time to learn about hospitals and machines, on this page, write or draw about what feelings you have had today – mad, sad, happy, scared – and any other questions or thoughts you may have since starting this book.

Today's date is _____

Help Me Understand... Death

The Heart

The heart is the part of our body that keeps us alive by pumping blood to the rest of our body. It is in the center of our chest protected beneath our ribcage.

As a reminder, many times people who go to the hospital come back home healthy. Sometimes when a person's heart stops working, doctors and nurses get it to start again.

Most of the time we draw pictures of hearts that look like this

But the heart inside our body really looks more like this

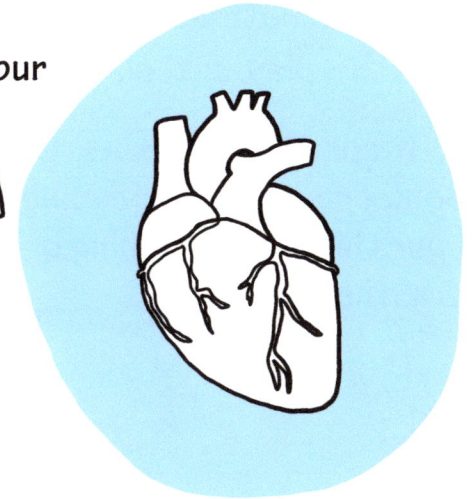

Make a drawing of a heart here:

Today's date is _____

The Brain

This is a drawing of the human brain colored for some of the different things the brain does.

The brain is what tells the rest of the body to do what it needs to do, like a computer has a brain that tells the keys and screen and programs to work. The brain is the part of the body that makes you feel emotions or pain in your body. It makes someone speak, breathe, play, eat, sleep, think, and all kinds of things.

Write or draw a picture about a time you remember speaking to someone, playing or eating with someone, or draw or write about your thinking, breathing or sleeping. These are all the things your brain helps you do.

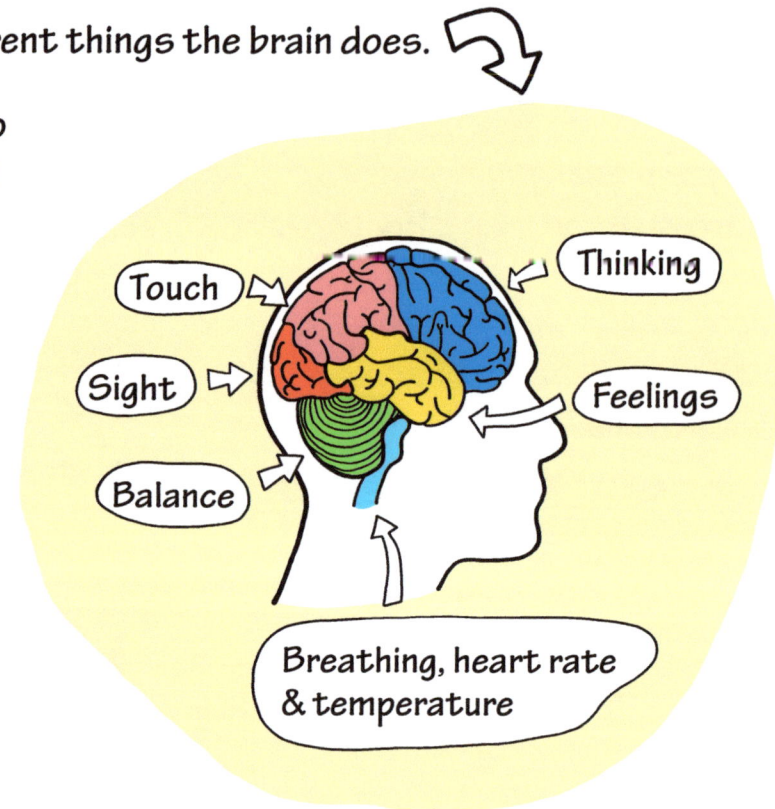

Touch

Sight

Balance

Thinking

Feelings

Breathing, heart rate & temperature

Today's date is _____

The Brain: Cranial Nerves

This is a picture of 4 of the 12 cranial (brain) nerves. The nerves are like wires that run from the brain to the rest of the body to help it do things. When the brain is working, people can do things like see, smell, chew/taste, and move their eyes side to side.

Draw a picture here of something you love to see or watch, something you like to smell, or something you like to eat or taste:

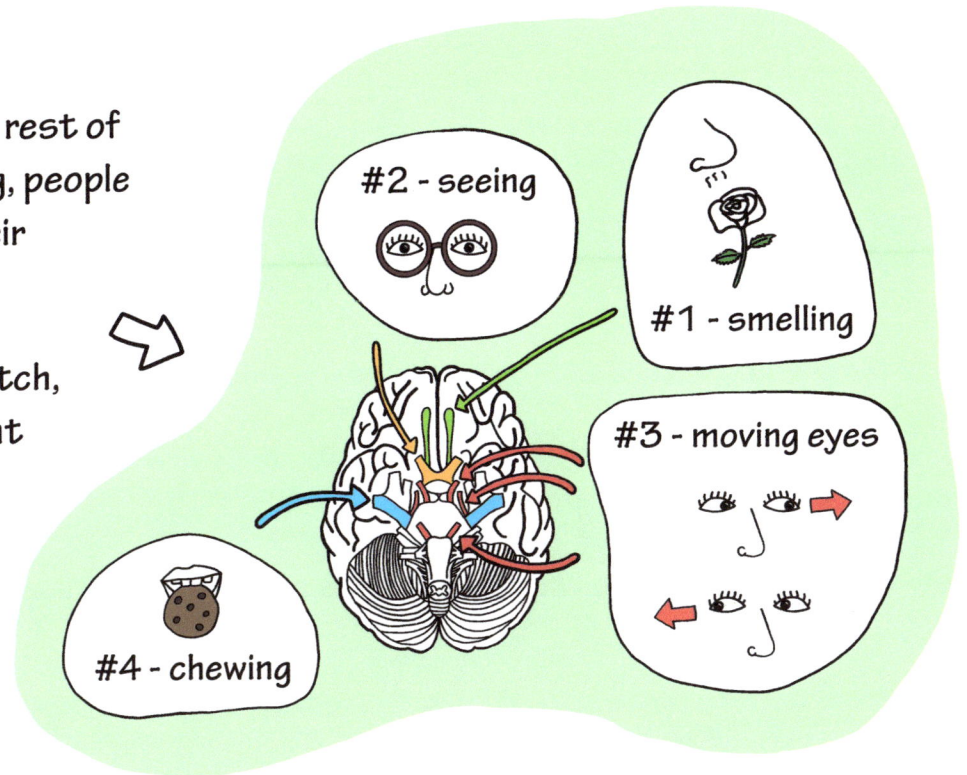

#2 - seeing

#1 - smelling

#3 - moving eyes

#4 - chewing

When the Heart Stops & Can't Start Again

Sometimes no matter how hard doctors and nurses try to make someone feel better, a person's heart can stop and can't be started again. When the person's heart can't be started again, the person dies. The person dies because when their heart stops working, the whole rest of their body (& brain) stops working. The blood stops being pumped by the heart, and in just a few minutes or hours their body can become cool to touch and firm or hard.

When someone dies, they don't feel any more fear or pain, they can't talk or dream or play or eat anymore.

Do you know someone who died because their heart stopped working? What questions do you have about this or how the heart works or stops?

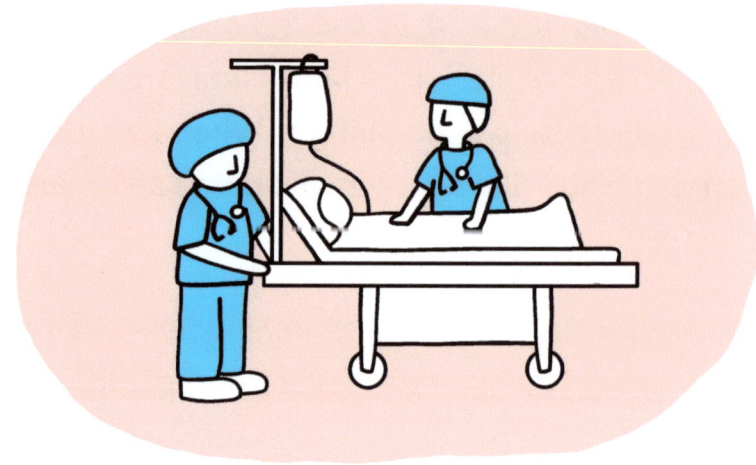

Today's date is _____

When the Brain Stops

Sometimes when a person dies, their brain stops before the rest of their body does. When the brain dies, it can't be started again, the person can't do anything, or feel any pain.

This is a picture of 4 of the cranial (brain nerves).

When someone is in a coma and cannot speak, 2 different doctors have to test these nerves at 2 different times to see if the brain is still working, and if the person is still alive. If even 1 cranial nerve is working, the person is alive. If none are working, the person is brain dead, not in a coma.

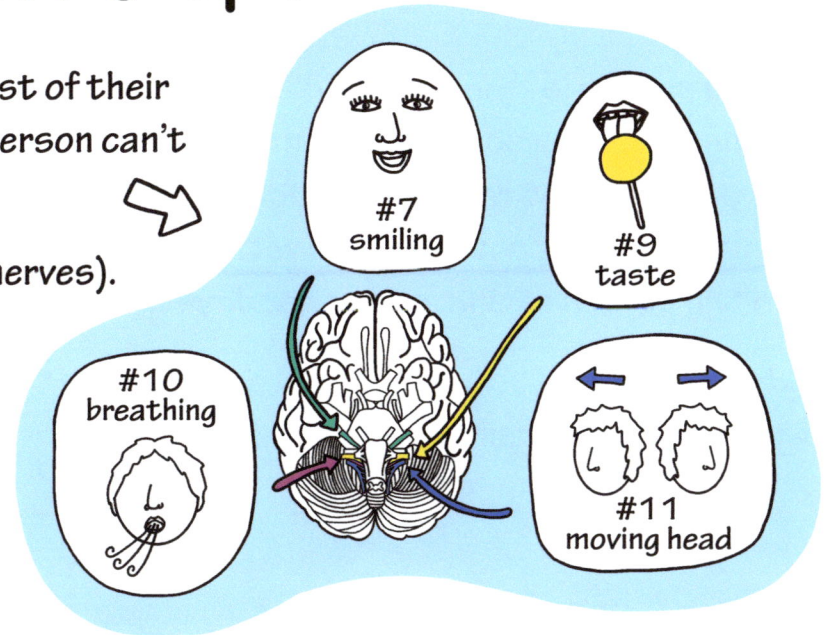

#7 smiling

#9 taste

#10 breathing

#11 moving head

Do you know someone who died because their brain stopped working? What questions do you have about this or how the brain works or stops?

Today's date is _____

The Dying Process: Saying Goodbye in the Hospital

When a person is dying or has died, and the person is connected to hospital machines, the person's body can look like he or she is sleeping and his or her body is still warm to the touch. Sometimes, this is when some family members like to come in and be with the person's body, or kiss the person, hold the person's hand, or say goodbye.

Did you come to the hospital and say goodbye to someone? Write or draw here what you remember doing or saying

Today's date is _____

The Dying Process: Saying Goodbye Now

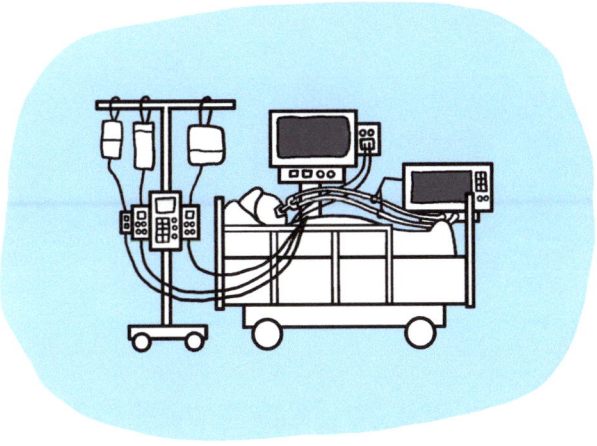

Some people don't like to see a person in the hospital when they are dying. Other people don't get a chance to visit the person in the hospital before they die. If you didn't want to, or didn't get a chance to, what would you want to say or do now? (Write or draw below)

Today's date is _____

Help Me Understand... Organ, Cornea, and Tissue Donation

Organ, Cornea, and Tissue Donation

Sometimes when a person dies, their organs or tissues can help someone else who is still alive.

But we don't mean organs, like the musical instrument

Or tissues like you blow your nose with

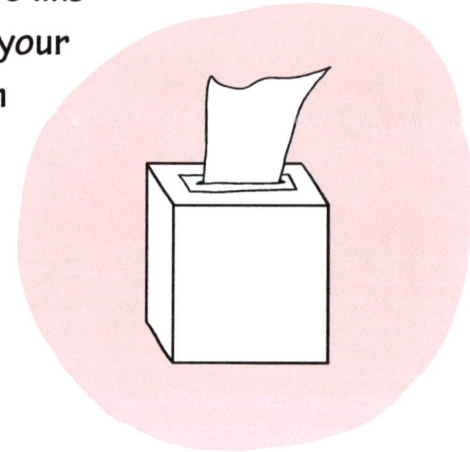

Do you know anyone who has donated organs, cornea or tissues? If so, write their name here and maybe any questions you have about this:

Today's date is _____

Cornea and Tissue Donation: Corneas

Corneas and tissues are parts of the body that can be surgically recovered or removed, then transplanted into someone else to help them live healthier lives. The tissues that can help others are corneas (the clear contact lens of the eye that can help people see), heart valves, veins, skin, and long bones of the arm or leg.

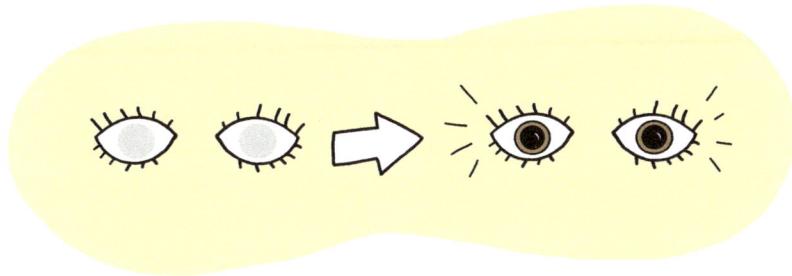

People with certain eye diseases like "Cataracts" and "Age-related Macular Degeneration" cause them not to see.

This little white line is the cornea: It is like a contact lens that helps people see.

Donated corneas help people see again. Do you know anyone who has donated cornea or tissues?
If so, write their name here and maybe any questions you have about this:

Today's date is _____

Cornea and Tissue Donation: Heart Valves

Heart valves are the little piece of the heart that works like a door to open and close and let blood flow in and out of the heart.

When someone's heart valves do not work, it stops the blood from getting to the rest of the body, and they need a surgery and new valves to help save their body. Who is alive in your life today that you love?
Draw or write about the people you love here:

Today's date is _____

Cornea and Tissue Donation: Veins

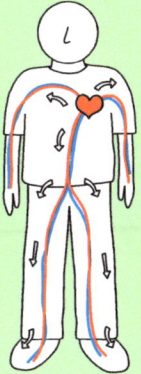

Veins are the tubes that help carry blood from the heart to the rest of the body to make it work, kind of like a hose carries water to help plants grow and live.

Donated veins can help people from losing their arm or leg.

Do you know anyone who donated veins after they died?
If so, write their name here:

Write or draw below some things you are grateful that your arms or legs do for you.
(Examples: running, walking, playing sports, waving, drawing, writing?)

Today's date is _____

Cornea and Tissue Donation: Skin

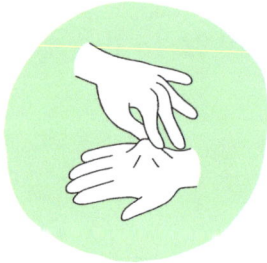

Skin is that stretchy stuff that covers your whole body. If you accidentally touch something sharp, you might get a cut in your skin. Sometimes if you get too much sun, you can get a sun burn on your skin. Sometimes if you touch something really, really hot, you can get a blister on your skin while it tries to heal.

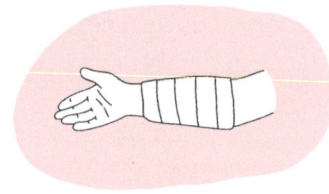

After someone dies, they can also donate some skin from special areas of their body to help other people who need skin to heal from burns, cuts, injuries, or surgeries.
Their donation is like a really special band aid.

Do you know anyone who donated skin after they died? If so, write their name here:
When was the last time you needed a band aid to help your skin heal? Write or draw that here:

Today's date is _____

42

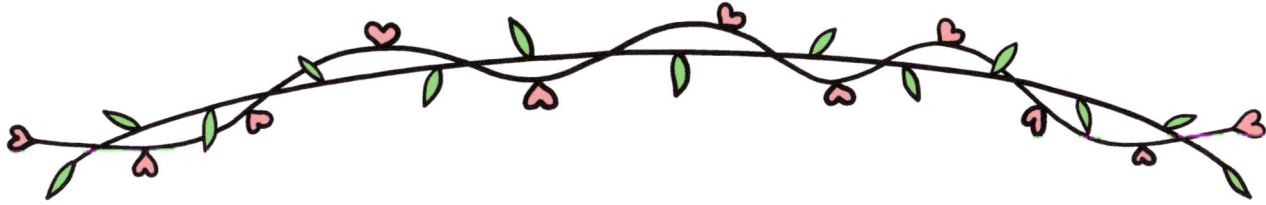

Cornea and Tissue Donation: Bones & Ligaments

After someone dies, they can donate the long bones and joint ligaments (the tissue that connects two bones together) to help other people. Bones and joints help people walk, sit, stand, run, play, and live.

Do you know anyone who donated bones or ligaments after they died?
If so, write their name here:

Write or draw some things here that you like to move around and do or play
(like skipping, soccer, jump rope, walking, wrestling, tickling):

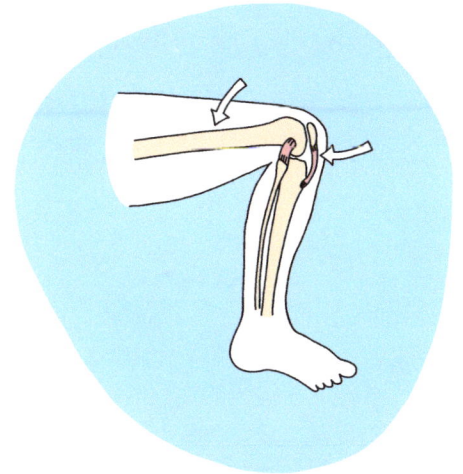

Today's date is _____

Organ Donation

After someone dies, they can also give the gift of vital organs to help others. The vital organs inside of a person who dies and is still on a ventilator that can be surgically removed (recovered) and transplanted into another person who is dying. These vital organs are another type of gift that can save the life of the dying person if they receive this transplant.

The organs that can be donated and transplanted are heart, lungs, kidneys, liver, small bowel, and pancreas. Here is what the heart, lungs and small intestines do:

2 lungs that breath oxygen

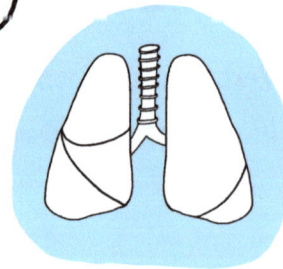

heart - which pumps our blood

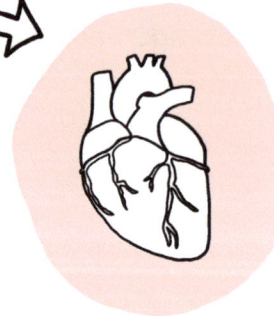

Do you know anyone who has donated heart, lungs or small intestines to anyone or anyone who needed a transplant to save their life? If so, write their name here and maybe any questions you have about this:

small intestine segment which helps us get vitamins and nutrients from our food

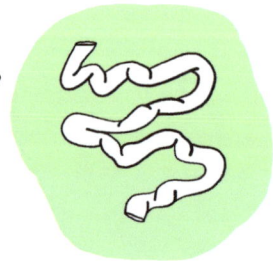

Today's date is _____

More on Organ Donation

Here is what the kidneys, liver and pancreas do:

2 kidneys that clean our blood and help us urinate (also called pee)

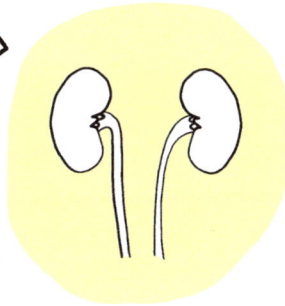

liver that cleans the blood and sometimes can be divided into 2 to save 2

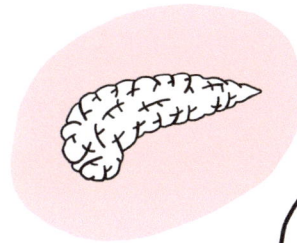

Do you know anyone who has donated kidneys, liver or pancreas or anyone who needed a transplant to save their life? If so, write their name here and maybe any questions you have about this:

pancreas - helps with digestion of food and keeps sugar levels in our blood balanced

Today's date is _____

Help Me Understand... What Happens Next

Funerals/Memorials

Ceremonies that honor and remember the person who died can help with grief in many ways.

What kind of ceremony or memorial did you have for the person who died?

Did you do anything at the ceremony?

Write or draw what you remember doing or feeling at the ceremony:

Today's date is _____

Funerals/Memorials: Memories

One of the ways ceremonies can help with grief is that people come together and tell stories and memories of the person who died. You can learn new things about the person. Story telling may feel both sad and comforting at the same time.

Write or draw one of your memories of the person who died here:

Today's date is _____

Funerals/Memorials: Support

Friends and family gather at ceremonies. Being together can feel supportive and that is another way ceremonies can help with grief. Write or draw or attach a photo of the people you like to be with who help you feel safe and supported:

Today's date is _____

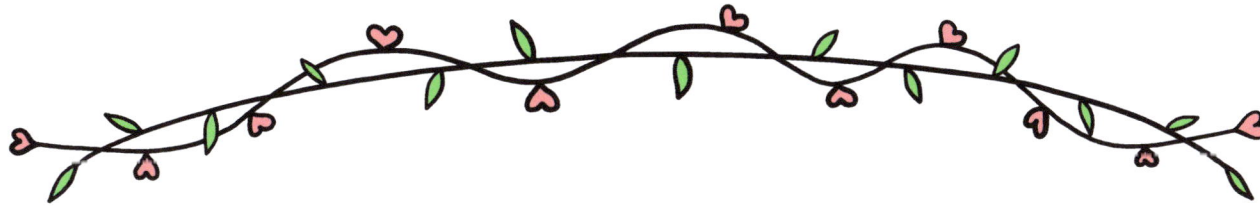

Funerals/Memorials: Future Rituals

Rituals are an action or several actions that can be done in the future to remember and honor someone who has died. These can help people remember the person who died and comfort people who are grieving. What would you like to do in the future to remember the person who died or to feel supported as you grieve? Circle any of the examples below that might help you, or write or draw other ideas of your own:

Getting helium filled balloons and writing special messages on the balloon and releasing them into the sky

Placing flowers on the ocean, lake, or river

Lighting a candle; and many, many more.

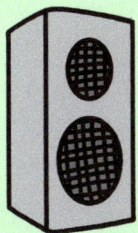

Playing their favorite music

Visiting their favorite restaurant or eating their favorite food in memory of your love for them

Getting a birthday cake on the person's birthday

Visiting the cemetery

Today's date is _____

Help Me Understand... Grief

Grief

Thoughts

Feelings

Thoughts and feelings can change a lot and very fast after someone close dies. These changes are called "grief" or "grieving". Sometimes you can feel many different feelings all at the same time, or have many thoughts all jumbled in your head when you are grieving.

Now that you have had some time to learn about how the body dies, on this page write or draw on about what feelings – mad, sad, happy, scared – you have today. Also, write or draw any other questions or thoughts you may have about dying, death, grief or grieving since your loved one died

Today's date is _____

Feelings Check

Mad

Sad

Angry

Happy

Relieved

Afraid

Scared

Again, just like things change in the weather, feelings continue to change over time and much faster than the weather or the seasons. Now that you have had some time to learn about death, donations, and grief, on this page, write or draw about what feelings you have today – mad, sad, happy, scared – add any other questions or thoughts you may since starting this book.

Today's date is _____

Coping

"Coping" is a word that people use to describe how you help yourself feel better or get through something difficult. There can be many ways to help yourself feel better, but each person is different. Circle some of the pictures below to show what helps you feel better:

Color

Look at pictures

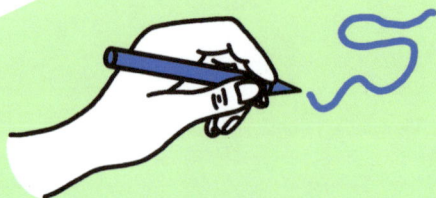

Take a walk in nature

Smell flowers

Breathe deeply and slowly

Make a craft

Get some sunshine

Today's date is _____

Coping

Fly a kite

Go running

Play in the leaves
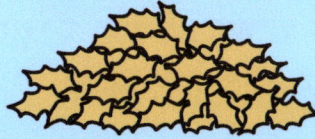

Climb a tree

Pet a furry creature

Watch a funny movie

Listen to music

Play a game

Swim in a pool

Journal

Talk to a friend

Today's date is _____

Who Can Help Me In The Future?

Now that we are nearing the end of this workbook, you may be wondering if your grief should be over. No. Grief is a long process and there is no right or wrong way to grieve. It's not your job to forget the person who died, and in fact "forgetting" is probably not a healthy goal. But, you will need to find people a long the way to help you with grief when you need it. These can be people in your family, friends, or other caring people. Some examples of caring people outside of your family are:

Teachers

Sports or Dance Coach or Music Leader

A counselor or therapist

Doctors and nurses

MATH

Who can you turn to for help when you need it? Write their names or draw them here:

Today's date is _____

Notes to Help Me Understand

Now that you have completed the book, write or draw out any other questions, memories, or thoughts that you would like to ask about or share with someone you trust.

Today's date is _____

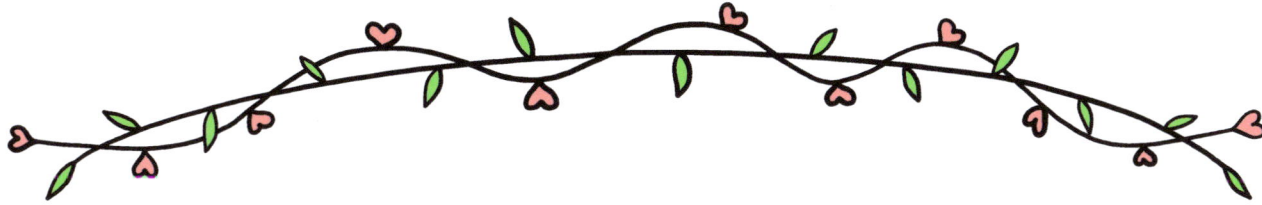

Closing note:

Thank you for finding this book. I hope you found it helpful. I imagine that some of the pages were easier than others to explain or complete. I know that it may not have covered everything you needed and welcome you to use it in conjunction with other great books like:

Fall of Freddie the Leaf by Leo Buscaglia, Ph.D (Poetic look at the life cycle and its meaning good for all ages)

Lifetimes: The beautiful way to explain death to children by B. Mellonie R.R. Ingpen, (Gentle explanations of the life cycle good for ages 3-7.

When Dinosaurs Die by Laurie Krasny Brown & Marc Brown (Book discusses all causes of death, what death is, and all customs around death using cartoon dinosaurs good for Ages 5-12).

Any number of books by Marge Heegaard:
- _When Someone Very Special Dies_ (Workbook format dealing with lifecycle, grief reactions, memories and coping strategies, - * in Spanish as Cuando Alguien Muy Especial Muere).
- _When a Family Is in Trouble: Children Can Cope With Grief from Drug and Alcohol Addiction._
- _When Someone Has a Very Serious Illness: Children Learn to Cope With Loss and Change._
- _When Something Terrible Happens_

If you need additional support, have questions, or wish to provide feedback for improvements to the book, please do not hesitate to reach out.

Sincerely,

- Michelle